YOUR WORK FROM HOME PRODUCTIVITY
HANDBOOK

How to stay healthy, happy,
and productive working from home,
even during a global pandemic

Tim Borys

ISBN: 978-0-9878148-9-0

Cover art by perfect_designx.
Layout by Kostiantyn Aksonov and Tim Borys
www.thefitnesscurveball.com
www.freshfitness.ca
www.timborys.com

Photos by Tim Borys, Krissie Eberhart, and Kate McKenzie

The dynamic nature of the internet precludes that web
addresses or links herein contained may change
after publication.

Edition: February 2021

TABLE OF CONTENTS

BEFORE WE BEGIN

While this document was designed as a "work-from-home" guide, it would be silly of me to not acknowledge the current situation we are dealing with.

This is the first time in history our global society has had to deal with a challenge of this scale. Because of these extraordinary circumstances, people are feeling abnormally elevated and prolonged levels of stress and uncertainty.

As this second edition is being published, we are almost one year into the global pandemic. Different countries, industry sectors, and people have had wildly varied experiences; but collectively, the toll on our overall health, well-being, and society has been massive.

Depending on your location, you may have experienced multiple "lockdowns", faced serious restrictions to work, family, and social schedules, endured the fear of illness, or even suffered the loss of family and friends to this virus. Thinking back to a year ago, it seems like a quaint notion that many people believed the social restrictions and work from home orders would last "a few months".

This "it will end soon" mentality has left many people still suffering and struggling to get by on a daily basis with their at-home work setup, and daily habits. Helping my clients not just "manage" but thrive through this challenging year has been a major focus for me and my team.

Sure, many companies have stepped up to provide better tools for workstation setup, access to periodic tip sheets, webinars, and various online resources. However, very few organizations have provided the tools, strategies, leadership support, and daily accountability that is needed to THRIVE during this work from home (WFH) phase of your career.

YOU are the architect of your own success, so if your company isn't providing the tools you need to succeed, going out and getting them yourself is a smart decision (and hopefully a key reason you bought this book)!

That brings me to the next important point.

The past year has fundamentally changed business and society. Yes, some things will revert closer to how they were before this pandemic, but many areas will continue changing rapidly.

The Future of Work

Work is one of those areas.

Of course, when it's safe to do so, many people will head back to the office. However, I believe the office of the future will be very different than it was a year ago.

There will be less people in the office, less often, companies will change how they utilize their existing real estate and use of online/digital platforms for work will continue to expand rapidly.

I foresee the majority of companies embracing a hybrid approach where employees come to the office part time and work remotely the remainder of the time.

The fact is, organizations have realized that most corporate work can be done from anywhere with an internet connection, and that when done right, remote work benefits both employees and companies.

This just means we have to be better at "doing remote work the right way!" This book is your handbook to do that.

The "work from home tips" we will discuss throughout this book are designed to set up your foundation for personal and professional performance. They cover the practical logistics of workspace, desk set-up and home environment, as well as the essential mental and physical aspects that allow you to perform at your best each day.

More about those aspects later, but first, for those of you that are (relatively) new to working from home, working from home is not "slacking", despite people falling into that mindset from time to time.

It may be different, but you can be just as productive and effective, if not more so, than you can in the office. That's assuming you apply and follow the tips we discuss in this book!

If you've been struggling with working from home, this book will be a lifeline to reframe, refocus, and reinvent your at-home work environment. **You have my permission to ENJOY working from home...AND to get more (of the right) SH!T done!** ☺

Let's be clear...this book is not meant as a comprehensive guide to every aspect of working from home. Each person's, home, and business setup are unique, and individual adaptations will need to be made to optimize how you work from home.

More simply, this book is a "quick reference guide" to the essential components you need to be healthy, maintain your energy, and continue being productive while working from home.

While some people have worked from home for ages and figured out ways to get the job done, the majority of our global corporate population is used to going into the office each day, having a proper desk setup, and working in a structured environment throughout the workday.

Leaving arguments aside about whether or not the traditional office environment is an ideal setup, we can likely agree that for most people, working from home requires a significant mental, physical, behavioural, and lifestyle adjustment.

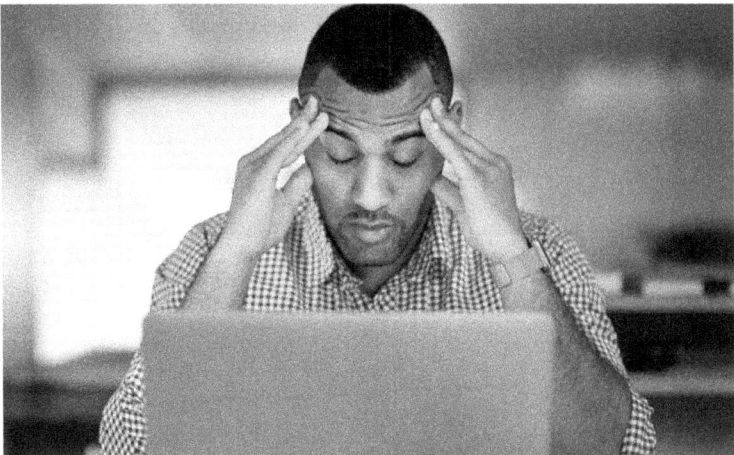

Combine this with the current climate of self-isolation, physical distancing, and stress generated by a global pandemic, and the tips in this book are even more important to our health, happiness, and personal performance.

Without these key aspects in place, your quality of work, health, happiness, and outcomes in life will continue to suffer.

Here's a quick summary of what we will cover in the coming chapters:
- Home office equipment and workstation setup
- Important ergonomic tips to avoid aches, pain, and injury
- Setting up your physical environment for success
- Scheduling, planning, and organizing essentials
- Productivity best practices
- How to work from home with a family and kids
- How to master your 4 Pillars of Personal Performance

Additionally, the mental and physical aspects of personal performance will significantly improve your ability to manage stress, anxiety, fear, and uncertainty, build resilience, and keep the rest of your life functioning well outside of work.

On these topics, we will cover:
- Creating (and following) a clear schedule for you and your family
- Movement, stretching, relaxation, breathing, and exercise
- Communication with friends, family, and loved ones
- The practice of daily gratitude
- Humour, laughter, and fun
- And much more

There's even a sample high performance daily "work from home" schedule to get you started. This is designed to help make it easier to modify it for your own needs.

After working with thousands of corporate clients both inside and outside the office, I can attest to the fact that these tips, guidelines, and schedules work. In fact, I routinely work from home, remote environments, and random places when traveling (remember what it was like to travel), and they have been indispensable for my personal performance and productivity.

I hope they work as well for you as they have for me and my clients. Now, it's time to dive in and get started towards positively transforming your work from home experience!

Yours in Health, Happiness, and Personal Performance
Tim Borys
CEO
FRESH! Wellness Group

YOUR EQUIPMENT NEEDS

Let's talk about the equipment you need to work successfully from home. Contrary to what many people think, it does not actually require that much. In fact, you likely have the essentials already.

My hope is that after almost a year of working from home, you have a decent setup, and that we can simply focus on optimizing that setup to improve your health and productivity.

However, it still shocks me how many people have spent the last year hunched over their laptop on the kitchen table or spend most of their day working from a laptop on the couch. This is a posture and performance nightmare, yet for many people it's still their daily reality.

For most people, this equipment needs section may seem fairly basic. That's OK, use it as a checklist or reminder that you've come a long way and have most of the pieces in place.

ESSENTIALS

Here are the absolute essentials you need to work from home...

- A flat surface to work from
- Internet Connection
- A device to access the internet

Even a chair and phone are optional (though you likely have those around your house already).

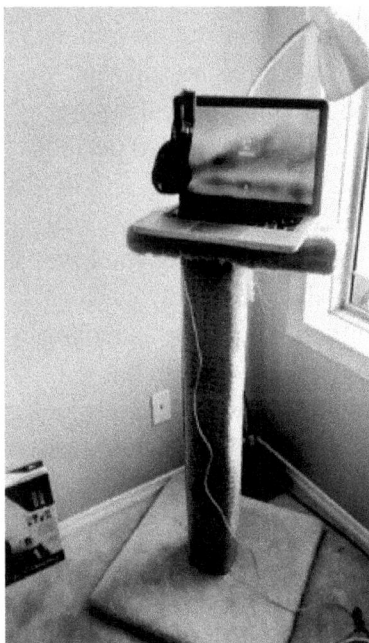

Here's a funny example that still works...well, maybe not for the cat!

My wife was using the home office for a meeting, and both of my kids were using the other two desks we had in this room. I still wanted to be near the kids to help with their homework but had no other place to work except the floor.

While hopefully you won't need to rely on your cat's scratching post, the goal is to show you that you don't need a fancy home office to be healthy and productive working from home.

Let's dive a little bit deeper into each of the essential tools.

For your flat surface, the kitchen table, counter, or even an old shelf or door between two side tables can work. As a standing workstation, you can use a chair on a table, stool on a counter, or a laptop or tablet on a dresser!

Your chair can be just a basic kitchen chair and doesn't have to be a special ergonomic model. An exercise ball is also a great option to keep your core connected and improve your alertness throughout the day. Just be sure that it's the right size for you (more on that later).

If you follow the movement tips we have later in this document, you will not be sitting for extended periods anyway.

The type of phone you have doesn't necessarily matter either. It could be a landline or a mobile phone. If it is a mobile phone, definitely look at whether you need to up-grade your plan to add more voice minutes.

I didn't think this would be an issue for me, but I ended up having to deal with it in an unexpected way.

The great thing about working from home is that you don't have to be at home. The same principles we cover in this book will allow you to work from anywhere.

My family likes to get out to the mountains, and we were spending several days each week away from home at a place in the mountains. This meant I found myself working semi-regularly from one of the local ski hills.

The lockdown and safety restrictions meant that we weren't able to use the lodge or access WIFI for more than a few minutes at a time. This forced me to rely on my phone and work from our car in the parking lot.

Not ideal, and I wasn't trying to do full days of work in this environment; but it allowed me to be in the same location as my family and partake in the mountain activities (skiing, fat biking, and hiking).

There were blocks of several hours each week where I was calling in, working from my laptop, and having to send documents. With poor reception, and minimal roaming data, it soon became clear that I needed to upgrade my mobile plan.

This was a simple fix that dramatically improved my ability to work from anywhere, but it wasn't something I initially considered.

At the most basic level, it's possible to work exclusively on your phone...though I don't recommend it from a sanity perspective!

Trying to work of such a small screen for prolonged times is not sustainable. Phones can be helpful for short, targeted tasks such as email, messaging, or sharing document links when you are away from your regular "office".

Of course, the ability to work from your phone depends largely on the type of work you are doing and which programs you need to access.

The best option would be to have a tablet, laptop, or a desktop computer. As long as you have a keyboard, internet connection and a screen, you can get work done.

As for your internet connection, the faster and more stable the better. If needed, call your internet service provider (ISP) to open more bandwidth. This should be a simple phone call and doesn't always require a service visit.

NICE TO HAVE ITEMS

Beyond the essentials, here are some "nice to have" items that will make your work from home experience more enjoyable (and perhaps a bit less painful):
- Additional monitor (particularly if working from a laptop or tablet)
- Wireless keyboard and mouse (great for using with a mobile phone, tablet or laptop to improve ergonomics)
- Headphones
- Multi-plug extension cord or power bar
- Chair with height adjustment

- Webcam on top of monitor
- An actual desk with drawers
- An exercise ball to sit on (and use for exercises and energy breaks throughout the day)

From an ergonomic perspective, an additional monitor is great. This is particularly true if you are working from a tablet or laptop.

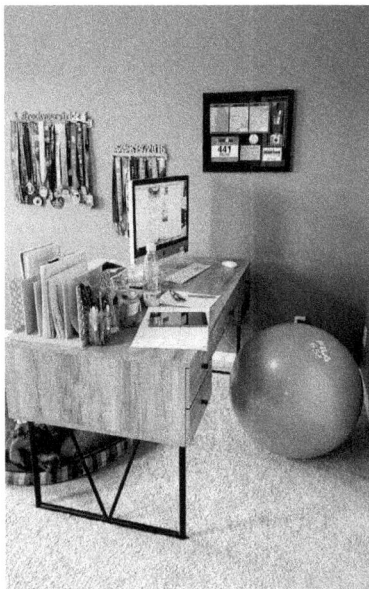

The alternative is to use a wireless keyboard and mouse to control your laptop, tablet, or phone so that the screen can be placed closer to neutral eye height when seated or standing. Read more about this in the "Important Ergonomics Tips" chapter.

If your additional monitor does not have a built-in camera, you can get some great quality external webcams that sit on top of any monitor. Having this feature is great for video calls because you can maintain proper head/neck position, and people on the call won't be looking up at the bottom of your chin as would happen when using a laptop camera.

(Note: using a wireless keyboard/mouse with your laptop or tablet solves this problem because the camera can be placed at proper monitor height while you control it via the keyboard and mouse)

These are not that expensive and can usually be delivered within a couple of days from Amazon. Almost all new ones will have high-definition quality. Of course, there are a lot of other "bells and whistles" you can get, but the basics are all you need.

If there are other people in your house, headphones work really well to cut down the noise from meetings, phone calls, and videos that you may be watching. The solution can be as simple as the earbuds from your phone.

"You will likely have a number of devices and electronic equipment to plug in, so it is great to have a power bar or a multiplug extension cord." Bonus if it has a surge protector!

While almost any flat surface will do, a formal desk is a nice bonus. Usually, they have drawers for storage so you can keep your desktop (and headspace) free of clutter!

If you can upgrade your chair a little bit, a basic office chair with height adjustment will come in handy to make sure you are set up in a better position to avoid neck aches, eye strain, and overuse injuries while seated.

An exercise ball is also a great option to keep your core connected and improve your alertness throughout the day. Just be sure that the angle of your thighs is well above parallel when seated. Ideally the angle of your knees should be 110-120 degrees.

If you want an even better setup, here are some options for you.

IDEAL SETUP

Your ideal home office set up may look like this, or it may be more customized to your specific needs. Keep in mind that these are NOT essential, so don't feel you need them to be able to work effectively from home. I worked from home for many years before having a separate office and a proper sit-stand desk.

These options are listed because they can help you be more productive, ease aches and pains, and create a more streamlined and seamless work from home experience.

- Adjustable sit/stand desk with keyboard and monitor height adjustments
- Ergonomic chair (along with a plan to stand/move at regular intervals)
- Height adjustable stool, "standing chair" or "perch"
- Anti-fatigue mat or Active Office Board™ for standing
- HD webcam with directional microphone for video conferencing
- Subscription to online video conferencing software service (ZOOM, GoToMeeting, etc.)
- Double or triple large monitors for segmenting information, workflows, and video conference feeds
- Separate, quiet office with a closed door and plenty of natural light
- Printer and scanner
- Wireless, noise cancelling headphones for conference calls, listening to music, or increasing task focus

I will remind you again...all of these above-mentioned items are optional, but when put to proper use they can make the working from home experience much more smooth and enjoyable.

Additionally, all fancy equipment in the world is useless if you don't have the other components of your environment, productivity, and personal performance plan in place.

These will be discussed in other chapters, but I want to mention it now because many people are quick to buy lots of equipment and think that's all they need. Your equipment is just one piece of the performance puzzle.

An adjustable sit/stand desk is one of the best investments you can make to avoid aches and pains while maintaining your energy throughout the day.

They come in all kinds of shapes and sizes, but the most important thing is to be able to adjust your working surface and monitor height to fit the ideal working position in either a seated or standing position.

Whether you choose a desk that raises and lowers, or a specialty unit that sits on a pre-existing desk will depend on your particular setup and what you currently have available. One isn't better than the other, they are just different.

The important thing to remember is that whether you are sitting or standing, being in a static position for a prolonged period of time is not good for your health and energy. Ideally, we are moving our body every 20 to 30 minutes. Even if it's only for 10-20 seconds at a time, it will make an incredible difference in how your body feels, your productivity, and your ability to maintain energy throughout the day.

If you don't have the budget to get a formal sit-stand desk option, it's simple to create your own makeshift standing workstation (much easier with a laptop or tablet than with a desktop).

Here are a few simple options I've done around my house.

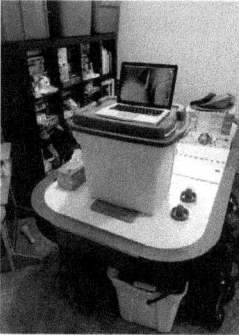

While many people are used to an ergonomic chair in the office, when proper movement and posture cues are remembered throughout the day, we find that fancy chairs aren't as necessary. However, if this is something you are used to, then by all means use one... as long as it's used properly.

I've personally found that a height adjustable bar stool or "standing chair" are most effective to use with a sit-stand desk.

While there are many specialty options costing $300-800 each, mine was $79 at a local big box store (on sale from $139) and has lasted me several years already. I just got a pair of new ones on Amazon for $159 (for both).

As mentioned in the "Nice to Have" section, an exercise ball is also a great alternative to traditional chairs. Just be sure it is large enough to keep your hips higher than your knees. It should also be burst resistant in case you roll over a staple, pushpin, or your pet pops it! A good quality burst resistant one will ensure you don't end up on your butt unexpectedly.

IMPORTANT: Not all exercise balls are the same! Quality is extremely important and low-quality balls are a massive safety risk. Check out www.freshfitness.ca/blog for an article I wrote that explains the risks and various quality levels. It's a quick read, and extremely worth it!

Anti-fatigue mats are another excellent way to keep your body feeling great throughout the day. You can buy special high density commercial ones or pick up a cool product like the Active Office Board from Fitterfirst.

If you're looking for a do-it-yourself option, folding over a yoga mat a few times, or standing on a folded towel can help. The essence is just to have something soft to take the pressure off your joints when standing for longer periods.

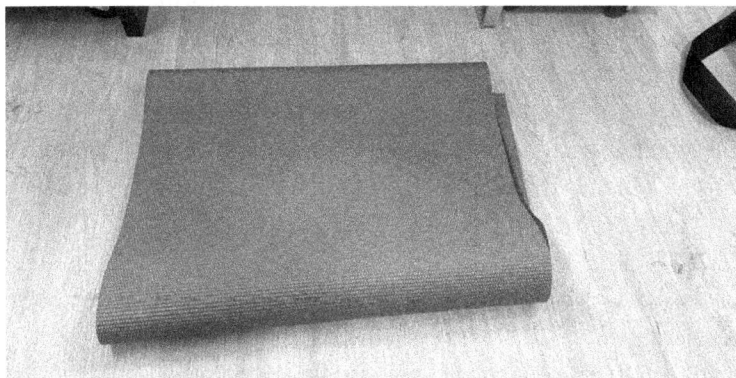

I won't go into detail on various webcams and microphones for video conferencing. These are specialty items, and you can find thousands of them on Amazon, Best Buy, or other online computer retailers search.

The same goes for video conferencing software. Many organizations already use specific tools such as Microsoft Teams®, GoToMeeting®, Zoom®, or many others. The ones you use will likely be specific to your corporate IT department, or the people you need to meet with.

As mentioned in the "nice to have" option, an additional monitor is excellent for managing various information and works well. Having a double or triple monitor setup is more specific to the type of work you are doing.

People in graphic design, video editing, and software development like to have the setup to improve their performance and productivity each day.

Many things can be done online, and don't require paper copies, but it is still handy to have a printer and scanner around your office if that's something you will need for your work.

A basic multi-function printer/copier/scanner is great, but for higher volume you may need something more robust. One of my favourite office tools is my Fujitsu ScanSnap for high-speed, high-quality scanning. It's saved me countless hours over the years and is still going strong.

Smartphones also have excellent scanning apps available, so when it comes to scanners this is another option to consider. For scanning receipts to my bookkeeper, I've used one called CamScanner Pro for years and it's amazing. It cost me about $3.50, which is a great deal for how often I use it!

Upgrading your earbuds to wireless, noise cancelling headphones for conference calls, listening to music, or increasing task focus is another component of an ideal setup that makes connecting to people and devices just a little bit easier. They also allow you freedom to move while on calls. :-)

IMPORTANT ERGONOMIC TIPS

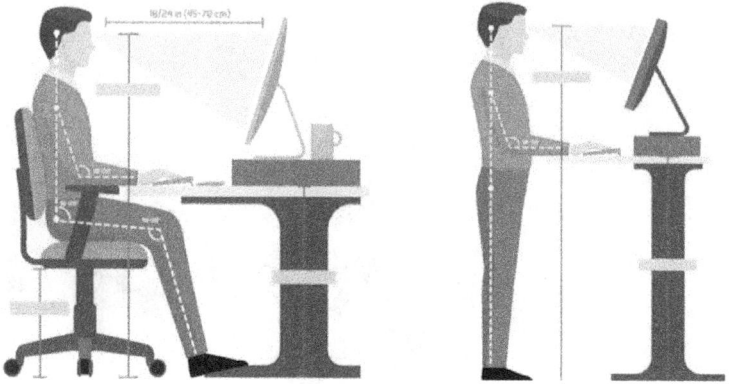

Even with the most basic equipment setup, you can still avoid aches and pains by following these simple ergonomic tips.

SITTING

- When you sit, sit with proper posture (see sample images)
- Stand up and move on a regular basis (aim for 30 seconds every 15 minutes)
- Screen height is extremely important to prevent neck strain. The top of your screen should be as close to eye height as possible (see posture and ergonomic setup images in this document for more specific cues)
- Elbows should be at or slightly above your keyboard height
- When standing, knees slightly bent and your pelvis in neutral position (think of your hips as a bucket of water, and try to avoid spilling any water over the front/back/sides of the bucket

STANDING

- Shoulders relaxed
- Maintain proper posture
- Keep your core engaged (at least around 20% effort)
- Ensure your pelvis is in neutral position (no spilling from bucket of water - see image)
- Move your legs every few minutes
- Raise one leg on a stool at times ("Captain Morgan" pose) - Alternate at regular intervals
- Hip/knee/ankle joints aligned (except when moving)
  o Applies to weight bearing leg when one leg is raised

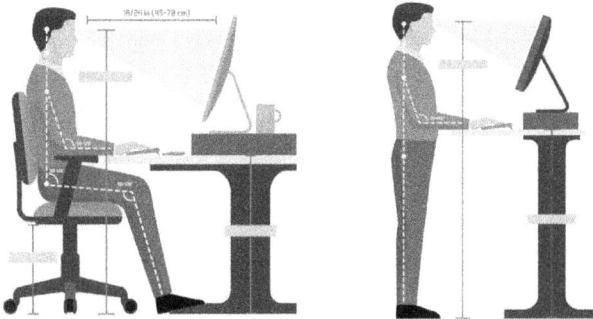

Bucket Analogy

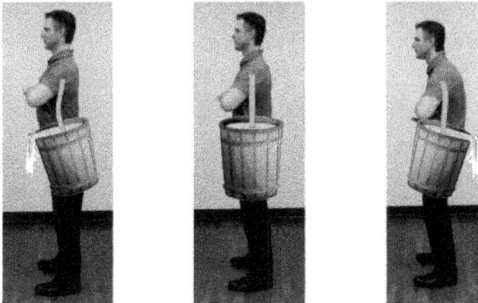

STAYING IN ONE POSITION FOR TOO LONG CREATES FATIGUE

- Move often and mobilize (take the joints in your body through their full range of motion on a regular basis)
- This improves blood flow, reduces fatigue, increases energy, alertness, and boosts your mood and critical thinking capabilities!

Here are some guidelines to consider that will help you set up your work environment in a more effective way, and minimize the aches, pains, fatigue, and overuse injuries that can come with either sitting or standing at a workstation.

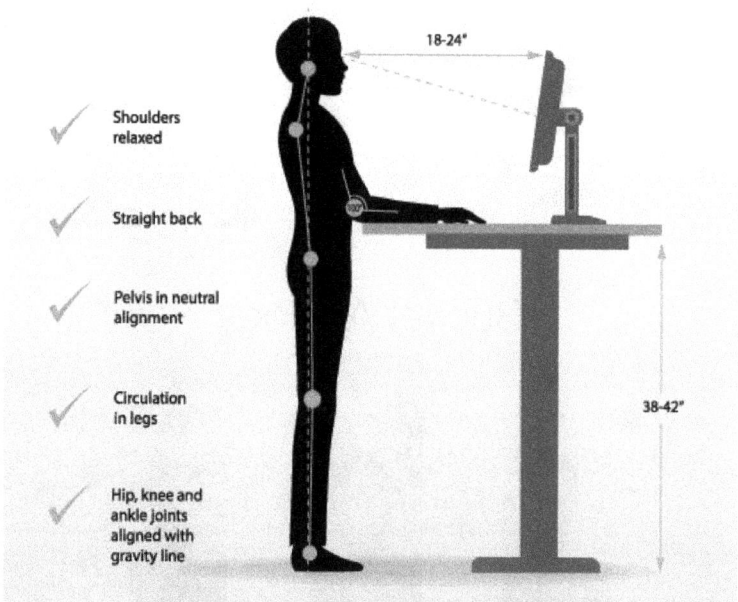

18-24"

✓ Shoulders relaxed

✓ Straight back

✓ Pelvis in neutral alignment

✓ Circulation in legs

✓ Hip, knee and ankle joints aligned with gravity line

38-42"

Regarding your foot position, the anti-fatigue mats mentioned earlier can be stood on (or your own homemade version).

YOUR WORK ENVIRONMENT

Now that we've talked about the equipment you need, let's move to where you will be working. Your environment is just as important as your equipment.

The first step is to create a quiet, distraction-free area you can use to work and conduct your meetings.

In a perfect world, it would be an office where you can close the door to minimize distractions. However, it could also be a space in your basement, living room, bonus room, bedroom, bathroom, kitchen, or any other place in your house that meets your needs at the time.

Whenever possible, set up your workstation near a window to get lots of natural light. This has a direct benefit on your health, mood, happiness, and overall well-being. If you can't do this, make sure to plan and take frequent breaks to get natural light throughout the day. This allows you to move at regular intervals, as well as get natural light. This tip is one of the best things you can do for your health and productivity each day.

With video conferencing in mind, look at where you set up your workstation. What will the background noise be like? What about the visual background? Are these factors conducive to video conferencing?

Turn on your webcam and look in the background behind you. clear out all personal items, mess, clutter, or distracting items. Try to set up your space so that other people won't be walking behind you when you are on a call.

Some great ways to do this include:

- Put up a nice poster or map on the wall behind you (the image below is from my friend Kate)
- Create a barrier between yourself and the rest of the room. This could include:
  - o A standing room divider or bookshelf that you can put behind your chair.
  - o Turning your desk so your back is to a wall
  - o Set up a makeshift backdrop by hanging a sheet over a portable clothes rack or a bar that's suspended between two poles.

Note that some video conferencing software systems like Zoom allow you to upload background images that will be placed behind you during calls.

This may require an upgraded subscription option and a more recent version of certain operating systems (my previous laptop was old and unable to take advantage of this feature, but it worked on my iPad).

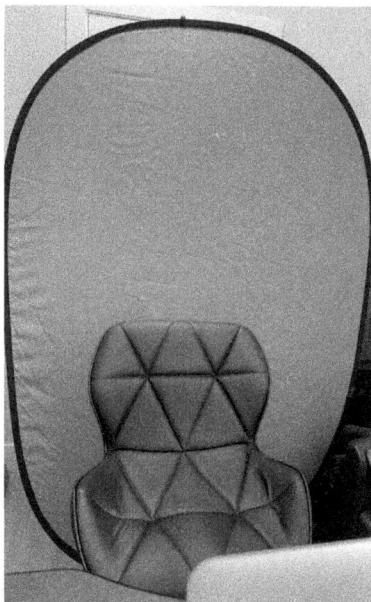

If you want to get a bit fancier and take better advantage of the virtual background feature, you can get a portable greenscreen.

These are reasonably priced on Amazon or from your local photography store and will open up a range of possibilities, including using your PowerPoint slides as a virtual background (a great way to spice up your presentations and meetings)!

SCHEDULE & PRODUCTIVITY

Scheduling Essentials

A solid schedule sets the foundation for your productivity. Routines are calming and centering, particularly during times of uncertainty and distress.

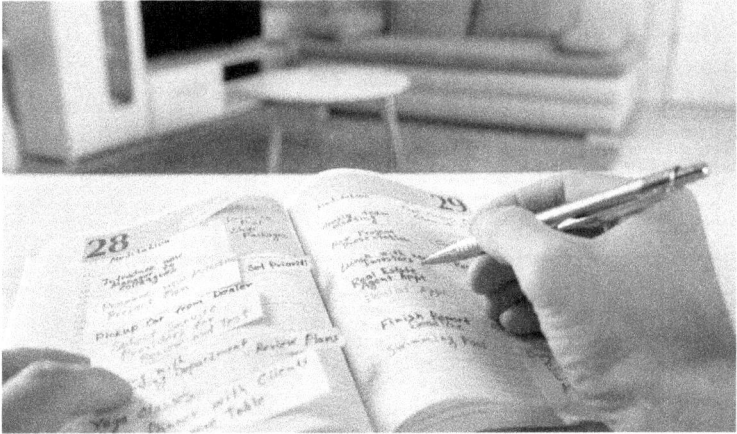

A productive routine will allow you to focus on what's needed most and assure the highest priority items get the attention they deserve... and are more likely to get completed!

It's important to plan a daily and weekly schedule coordinate with everyone else in the house. Plan and share resources as needed. This will ensure any conflicts are avoided and everyone is on the same page. It also allows you to plan for time together so you can maximize your personal and business enjoyment.

A structured daily planner is ideal, but even a neatly written post-it note or sheet of paper will work. I find writing my daily plan and objectives down by hand to be useful, though it can be duplicated on a computer calendar.

While science has not proven it, there seems to be much anecdotal evidence (and corroborated by my personal experience over many years) that writing your daily goals and objectives by hand makes them MUCH more likely to happen. Another helpful tool is "time blocking." This means having clearly delineated times for key activities throughout the day.

A subset of time blocking is "batching" tasks. This means doing a bunch of the same type of task at the same time to maximize efficiency and resources. For example, check your emails at specific times each day, block off a set time period for social media responses, and have a set time to make/return phone calls.

These options apply to both work and personal times and they minimize the distraction and wasted focus that come with switching tasks repeatedly in a short period of time.

Look at all the items you have to get done each day, prioritize which are most important, estimate how long each will take, and allocate time in your schedule for the TOP 3 most important tasks. Other tasks will fit in around them.

To paraphrase Stephen Covey, if you don't consciously make time for and schedule the "Big Rocks" in your life, there will never seem to be time for them.

By defining what's most important to you in life (Your 'Big Rocks'), you can strategically schedule time in your days/weeks/months to ensure they happen.

Be sure to leave room for work, personal tasks, physical activity, productivity breaks, food, mental health time, and anything else you need to get done.

Schedule the "Big Rocks"

Instead of "sorting gravel"

Ensure other household members are aware of your schedule and needs during work time, particularly with regards to video conferencing or meetings.

PLAN and SCHEDULE the following tasks into your schedule each day.

Morning Routine

Allocate anywhere from 10-60 minutes to set your mindset, body, and energy up for a successful, high-performing day. In my book, The Fitness Curveball, there's an entire chapter devoted to structuring a successful morning routine.

Everyone's routine will be slightly different, but the key components are silence, mindfulness/breathing, movement, affirmations, visualizations, goals, and learning/personal development.

The key components of the FRESH! Start Morning Method™

- **Start** (Up, Prep and Doing).
- **Breathe** (Silence, Connect Body / Mind).
- **Speak** (Positivity, Affirmations, Goals).
- **Move** (Mobility, Exercise, SMR, Stretching).
- **Write** (Journal, Gratitude, Goals).
- **See** (Visualize, Goals, Day, Success).
- **Learn** (Read, Listen).
- **Go** (Shower, Dress, Eat).

If that seems too daunting...here's a simplified version.

- **UP** (1 - 5 minutes)
  - o Get up, find an open, quiet, uninterrupted space in your house
- **MOVE** (1 - 20 minutes)
  - o Mobility/Stretching/Exercise
- **BREATH** (1 - 20 minutes)
  - o Sit or stand in silence, breathe deeply, and embrace the quiet in your mind, body, and environment
- **MOTIVATE** (1 - 20 minutes)
  - o Journal, learn, get inspired, review goals, affirmations
- **GO** (variable)
  - o Shower, get dressed, eat a healthy breakfast, and transition to work mode

Whichever option you choose, be sure to get up 20-60 minutes earlier than usual (this is paired with going to bed 20-60 minutes earlier the night before).

Your time and focus may change each morning, but get each category done for at least 1 minute.

Workday Startup Routine

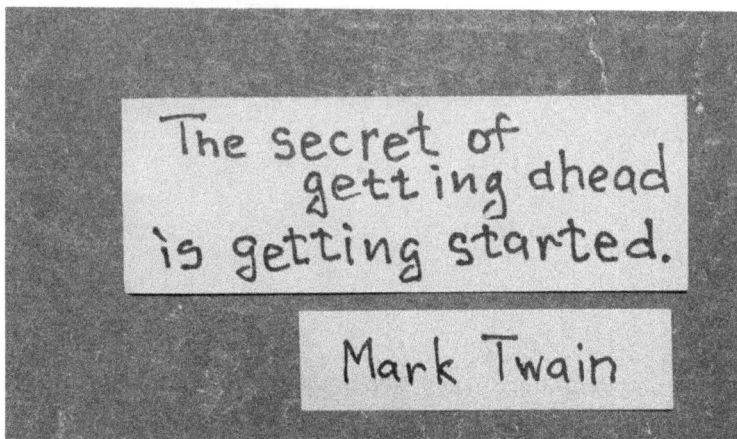

> The secret of getting ahead is getting started.
>
> Mark Twain

This is the first few minutes of your workday (usually 10-30 minutes) that set yourself up for productivity and success. Think of it as your morning routine for work.

It's during this time that we perform the basic tasks that need to be dealt with to keep us moving forward in the day.

Often these are things that will lead to interruptions, distractions or "fires" later in day if they aren't dealt with. By doing them early, we can anticipate and avoid much of the later impact.

Examples of tasks in your Workday Startup Routine are:

- Check-in with team/manager (daily stand-up meeting)
- Identify and request information that may be needed to do a later task or remove a key barrier to getting that task done.
- Review your daily Top 3 tasks

Workday Shutdown Routine

Again, this is 10-30 minutes at the end of each workday that sets you up for a successful and relaxing evening. It will help you avoid bringing work "home" and interrupting family or fun time.

Examples of common tasks include:

- Empty your email inbox of key responses that need attention (*this doesn't mean you have to clean everything out or deal with ALL tasks. Just the most important ones*).
- Review your weekly Top 3 tasks to see if you are still on track and make necessary adjustments.
- Review your accomplishments for the day
- Create your daily top 3 for tomorrow...and WRITE THEM DOWN. *Ideally in a structured daily planner, but even on a post-it note will make a positive difference.*
- Leave tomorrow's top 3 tasks open on your desk so it's the first thing you see when you start work in the morning.

- Shut down your computer and devices before leaving "work".

Even if you are literally walking to the next room, it's a psychological shift. Some people even go outside and walk around the block to "commute home" from work. :-)

FAMILY CONSIDERATIONS

Much of this section relates to children, however, many of the concepts (communication, scheduling, support, etc.) transfer well to ANY other people you may have in your home.

Whether you are caring for aging parents, living in a multi-generational household, have roommates, or just guests that are staying a while, it's still possible to set boundaries, establish schedules, communicate your needs, and get your work done with focus, efficiency, and effectiveness.

If you have kids that will be home when you are working, it's helpful to ensure they also have a schedule with clearly delineated times for age-appropriate learning and activities.

Over the past year, parents have also realized that they can't necessarily rely on schools to be open all the time.

With government stay-at-home orders, region wide school closures, and class quarantine measures, parents are having to contend with even school aged kids being home unexpectedly.

Having a plan and systems in place to manage these and other likely scenarios will help you mentally and physically when such times arise.

Keep in mind that expectations and activities will vary greatly based on the age of your children, their past experiences, and individual personalities.

If your children require more hands-on attention, plan a schedule with your spouse, partner, or another caregiver.

If you are a single parent, alone at home, and still need to work, work times may need to be shifted to accommodate the needs of your children.

Potential solutions are to coordinate video engagement with the child from someone off-site (Skype story time, remote teaching/tutoring, or craft projects).

In times like this, a virtual nanny share with another single parent may even be an option. As the saying goes, necessity is the mother of invention!

The goal is to carve out some quiet, focussed, productivity time for you to get your work done... and some to manage your mental health.

If you don't have childcare, you won't be as productive with work tasks when your child is around. This is a simple reality that many people struggle to accept.

It's important to manage your expectations early in the planning process and to identify times of high and low productivity based on your childcare schedule.

With young kids, it may be that the only time you can dive into work is at nap time or after they are asleep for the night. Regardless of your situation, the important part is to be honest about what you can realistically accomplish in a given time, while being sustainable over the long term.

Sure, there are times when you push harder, or burn the candle at both ends, but these should be short bursts, followed by clear periods of recovery.

Mental and physical energy need regular renewal.

Staying healthy, happy, and productive over the long term involves curating solid sources of positivity in your life, setting goals based on the "Big Rocks" in your life, reviewing those goals each day, getting a restful sleep most nights, getting ample amounts of physical activity.

Without ensuring these things are in place, we leave ourselves open to more stress, frustration, burnout, poor productivity, low energy and depressed moods. This is just the beginning and things only get worse if left unchecked.

If time is at a premium (and let's face it, it usually is when you have kids), taking care of your physical health by getting some activity can be done with your child. This can even be as simple as an impromptu dance party.

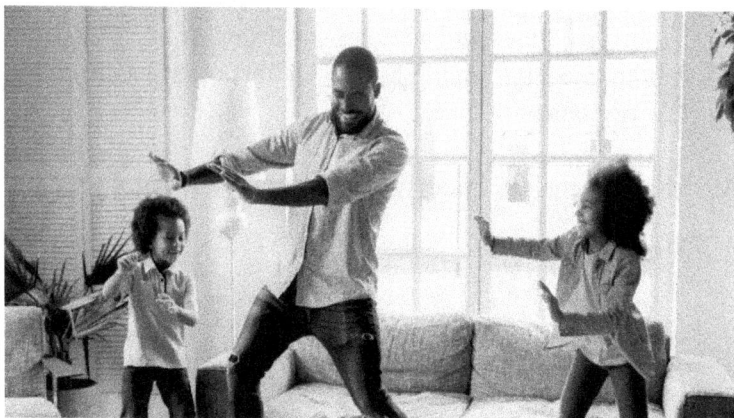

Plus, this is an excellent way to set a precedent and be a positive role model for healthy change in your child's life. It also maximizes your time and can be used for work/study breaks throughout the day.

NOTE: *There are lots of great exercise programs that are simple and can be done with kids – if you need some ideas or guidance, just reach out by email or social channels and I can send you some resources.*

The key here is to understand your unique situation and set your expectations appropriately. This is also important to communicate with your company and team, so they can help in the best way possible.

PRODUCTIVITY TIPS & BEST PRACTICES

This is where the rubber hits the road, and we optimize how much we are able to get done.

Working from home requires getting in the right mindset and transitioning from "home" to "work" each morning and back again in the evening.

If you've been working from home for any amount of time over the past year, you've likely fallen into a number of routines in your day and life. Some are positive, some are neutral, and others are negative or destructive

The good news is that you've made it through the past year of remote work and are reading this book, so at least some things are going well.

The question then becomes, are you merely "getting by", or are you "happily thriving". Far too many people I've met and spoken with over the past year are just "getting by", if not worse. They continue to "gut it out" each day, hoping for a "return to normal" sometime soon.

I'm a firm believer that life should be more than just "getting by", and as mentioned earlier, society and work likely won't return to how they were before this pandemic, so wishing for something that is unlikely to happen isn't helpful.

With that being said, there are a number of simple and highly effective ways we can TAKE CONTROL over our environment, systems, strategies, and actions each day to set ourselves up for greater success, health, and happiness.

The things we will cover aren't rocket science. Some may be new, and some you've probably already heard of.

You may have even tried some of these ideas in the past, but for some reason you stopped using them. Knowing why is important.

Did something come up that got you off track? After testing and tweaking your approach, did you determine it was ineffective?

to be best in any r
point of view.
System
group of intera
elements for mir
organized set o

The most important question is...are you using some type of system consistently and monitoring your progress to see if it's working?

This is important. Whether or not you use the ideas I have provided is less important than finding some type of system and following it consistently enough to determine if it's working.

From my direct personal experience and from working with thousands of clients over the past few decades, I can honestly say that a solid morning and evening routine (as described earlier) or two of the most beneficial (yet neglected) productivity and performance tips available.

Get up, drink a glass of water, then invest a few minutes in physically moving and motivating yourself for the day. Finally, shower, eat some healthy food and get ready for work.

If you normally wear business clothes, put them on. This alone is a huge psychological performance boost.

Yes, it's tempting to crawl out of bed, stumble downstairs to the coffee pot in your pyjamas, and log into your first meeting (with the video off) while hoping the caffeine kicks in soon. Resist this temptation, and plan ahead to avoid it by structuring your evening for a good night of sleep!

For the actual work part of your day, we will cover several simple and effective techniques in this next section.

Keep in mind that if you are exhausted, scattered, and unmotivated, these tips may still help, but will never maximize their (or your) potential.

I also want you to know that I'm not throwing random tips out there or speaking theoretically. I've lived and learned from EVERY one of the tips in this book, whether personally or through clients.

Those who know me well will tell you that I am notorious for "chasing squirrels" or indulging the whims of my "monkey brain". My wife would say I am "scattered" in these situations.

On the positive side of this personal trait is a non-linear creative brain that can come up with great ideas and see opportunities from unique perspectives.

On the negative side, if I fail to reign in and focus my scattered thoughts means I can get lost in my head with unrelated thoughts and end up getting very little accomplished of the things I was supposed to be doing.

Sometimes I will get to the end of a day having done 5% of 20 tasks, instead of 100% of the most important task.

Throughout my personal development journey and from working with various experts, I've learned many strategies that produce great results with less effort.

On that note, one of the my one of the most helpful techniques I've learned is The Pomodoro Method.

THE POMODORO METHOD

Normally the goal is to complete a certain number of work:rest cycles each day.

To use this technique:
- Decide on a specific task that you want to accomplish.
- Break down your task into smaller items that will fit within your desired work interval length (I typically do 30-45 minutes).
- Set a timer for the specific length of time and start working.

Working in set chunks of time with regular short rest breaks will allow you to focus on a specific task and provides a natural opportunity for a brain/body break to transition tasks (or come back to the same task with renewed focus and enthusiasm).

PARKINSON'S LAW

This is another strategy I've used (often in conjunction with The Pomodoro Method) to get more done in less time.

During grade school, university, and the start of my professional career, I almost always waited until the last minute to get assignments/projects/proposals done. It was the classic "procrastinate until the night before and then pull an all-nighter to get the assignment done".

For many reasons, this doesn't work well in adult life, especially when you have kids! However, this common experience is Parkinson's law in action. Most people have experienced it at some point in life.

Parkinson's law states that a task will expand to fill the time you allocate to it.

If you have a week to get something done, it will take you a week. Yet, much of the time during this week will often be wasted. However, if you only have an hour to get that same task done, you will have to drill down and focus on the most essential elements and get them done.

This is an extreme example, but hopefully you get the idea.

By forcing yourself into a time box, you are able to focus more effectively and challenge yourself to get more done in less time.

To simplify the approach, if you break a task down into manageable bites, and then set timelines for each, you are more likely to stay on track, avoid getting distracted, and get more done in less time.

I find having a timer visible helps me re-focus and get back on track when my mind starts wandering, or I get distracted (Look...a squirrel!).

Taking small breaks between work intervals gives your mind a rest and helps you transition between tasks.

SCHEDULE AN END TIME

Since this pandemic started, those working from home have found out what remote workers and business owners have always known...

Work is ALWAYS there until you shut it off!

Working from home is great in that it cuts down the commute, but this is one of the biggest downsides that must be managed for health, happiness, and success.

With this in mind, one of the best strategies is to set an END TIME FOR WORK TASKS, and your WORK DAY.

This sounds simple in principle, but it's much more challenging in practice. I KNOW the thoughts going through your mind..."I will just send this ONE email", or "I've got a few spare minutes, I may as well do a quick update to that spreadsheet".

As I know too well, there's always something that can be worked on, or something that didn't get resolved during the day. The goal is to set an end time to your day...and STICK TO IT.

Avoid letting work creep into your personal time. You need that "down time" for rest, regeneration, and recovery.

This is critical when working from home since we do not have the traditional office and home separation. The Workday Closeout Routine mentioned earlier is a great way to make this happen! Schedule it in your day with reminders.

Some people find it helpful to shut down and put away all their work items and do a "mental commute".

In practice, this can look like: finish work, put on your coat and walk around the block (literally) before coming back into the house and starting your personal/family time.

For added flair if people are home, you can warmly greet them with "Hi, I'm home!" when you arrive.

This is a great signal to your brain, and your family that there's been a transition from work life to home life.

If you are coming home to an empty house, a transition option is to call a friend for a casual chat as you start evening.

Another great option is to get some exercise!

This leads us into the personal performance section and one of the most often overlooked aspects of health and work productivity.

PERSONAL PERFORMANCE = WORK PERFORMANCE

The scheduling and productivity tips we've already discussed are components of personal performance, but these tactics won't be as effective if your brain and body aren't functioning at their best.

By ensuring that your health and energy are top-of-mind each day and that strategies and tactics have been planned into your schedule to maximize these areas, you will be able to better utilize your productivity tips and work environment.

Here are a series of tips that my coaching team and I have used successfully to help thousands of clients perform better at both work and home.

None of them are complicated, and I guarantee you've heard many of them.

However, despite "knowing" about these concepts, very few people actually perform the actions on a consistent basis.

This means they fail to reap the incredible rewards of these simple and highly effective habits.

The following section follows my 4 Pillars of Personal Performance Model. In order of importance, the 4 pillars are: Mindset, Habits, Movement, Fuel.

Because it's meant as a quick reference resource, I've kept it the details as a series of bullet lists.

Don't let the informal nature fool you. These are POWERFUL tips...when implemented.

Like some of the previously covered information, you may be tempted to dismiss some points as "too simple to make a difference".

I recommend rethinking that approach. Put these tips into action consistently and you will notice a tremendous improvement in almost every aspect of your life.

If you are struggling with the implementation process...AS FOR HELP! Whether from me, my team, or another professional, putting the tips into action is critical.

MINDSET

- Write down 3 things you were grateful that day. Do this before going to bed.
- Write down one challenge that you have & plan how you will seek support for it.
- Randomly compliment 2 people you know each day.
  - o Be specific and tell them how much you appreciate them or what they did.
- Answer these two questions:
  - o What was your greatest PERSONAL win today?
  - o What was your greatest PROFESSIONAL win today?

Choose your information sources.

News:
- Pick a max of 3 trusted and accurate news sources for updates and set specific times to check them each day (as part of your daily schedule).
- Set a time limit on how long you spend reading the news.
- Purposefully curate some POSITIVE news sources to balance out the negativity and anxiety provoking aspect of most news.
- Turn off notifications on your devices for news and social media (calls and texts are still ok. You can even

add specific people to a VIP list that will come through your notification blocks).

People:

Some people are "Negative Nellie's" and constantly see the world through a lens of negativity/pessimism.

- Intentionally limit your contact with these people, and instead choose to connect more with smart, thought-ful people who are choosing to see things through a more positive lens.
- This doesn't mean we avoid or forget the challenges we are facing. Rather, we choose to see them from a per-spective of adversity, challenge, and potential growth.
- There are MANY positive aspects of our current situa-tion (along with some negative ones), but most people will gravitate overwhelmingly to the negative.
- Our goal is to balance out that perspective so we can continue being happy, healthy, and performing at our best.

Social Media:

- As an extension of the news and people aspect, care-fully monitor your social media use
- Limit time on each platform
- Consciously search for positive posts
- Limit your access and time spent reading reactionary and overly pessimistic feeds and people
- Post positivity, helpful tips, and opinions or comments that will raise people up, help them succeed, and make the world a better place.
  o There are far too many trolls in the world already,

making yourself one of them won't help anyone, particularly you!

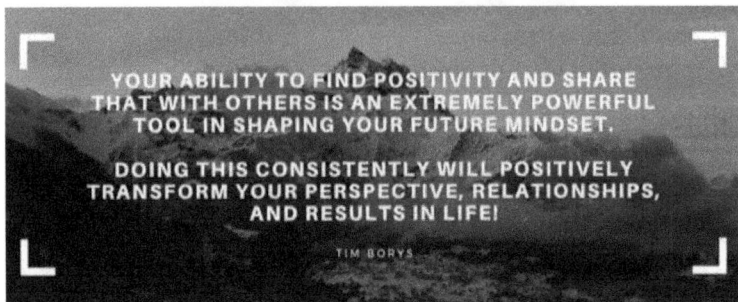

YOUR ABILITY TO FIND POSITIVITY AND SHARE
THAT WITH OTHERS IS AN EXTREMELY POWERFUL
TOOL IN SHAPING YOUR FUTURE MINDSET.

DOING THIS CONSISTENTLY WILL POSITIVELY
TRANSFORM YOUR PERSPECTIVE, RELATIONSHIPS,
AND RESULTS IN LIFE!

TIM BORYS

HABITS

- Establish a high performance morning routine:
  - o Movement, breathing, visualization, affirmations, goals review, learning, etc.
- Wake up and get ready like a regular work day.
  - o It's not helpful to stay in your PJ's all day!
- Connect via video with someone at work.
- Connect via video with someone outside of work (family, friends, etc.).
- End your work day at a specified time so you can transition to life outside work.
- SLEEP well. It is the most underrated aspect of health and the foundation for your energy, mood, and mindset the following day.

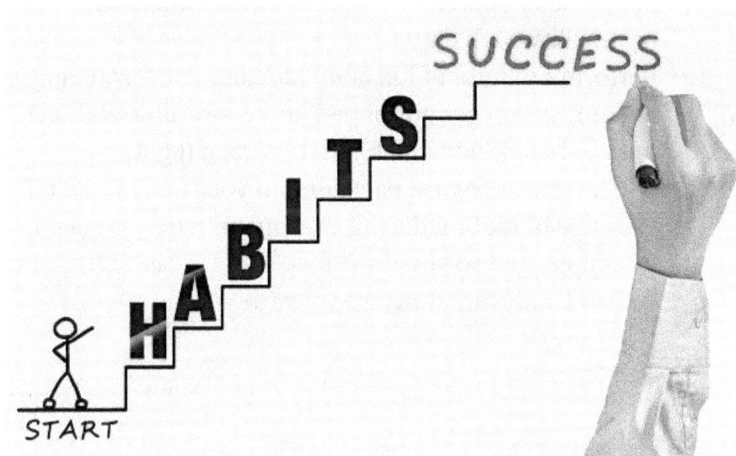

MOVEMENT

- Stand up and stretch for 30-60 seconds every 30 minutes.
  - o If you are using Pomodoro timers, use your short breaks to move your body for 1-2 out of the 5 minutes.
- Schedule a 20+ minute sweat session each day (and complete it).
  - o Simple bodyweight calisthenics are a great option. If you have more equipment, that works too.
- After each meal, walk around the block. Breathe deeply and enjoy the fresh air! This should take about 5 minutes. You can always go for longer if you desire.
- Complete at least two 5 minute movement breaks in the day.
- Schedule 10+ minutes of foam rolling, stretching and/ or mobility each day.
- Perform 1 minute of full body Mobility and stretching as soon as you get out of bed in the morning, and one minute before you climb into bed each night.
  - o The goal is to take each joint in your body to its full range of motion during that one minute. To keep it simple, and so you don't forget any areas, start your head and work down to your toes.

SUCCESS ISN'T ABOUT WHAT YOU DO IN THE GYM.

IT'S ABOUT WHAT YOU DO THE "OTHER 165 HOURS" EACH WEEK.
Tim Borys

FUEL

- Eat healthy, nutritious food at regular intervals throughout the day.
  - o Choose mostly fresh vegetables and fresh fruit with mean high quality protein sources
  - o Minimize sugar, processed foods, alcohol, and excess treats
  - o Small, high quality indulgences are great. they just shouldn't become the norm
  - o Limit coffee and empty calorie drinks (soda, juice, energy drinks, etc.)

Sesame Street has one of the best nutrition philosophies out there. It's easy for everyone to understand. Here it is in all its glory...

There are "Anytime Foods" and "Sometimes Foods."

We all know which foods fall into each category. People run into problems when "Sometimes Foods" become "Anytime Foods." That's it. Nutrition is really that simple!

- Establish regular eating and snack times and avoid food consumption outside those times.
- Make sure snacks and lunches are planned a day ahead, you could make this plan during dinner each night. To make it simple, this can even be leftovers

from that night's dinner.
- Listen to your body. It will tell you how it's responding to the food you eat. Eat food that makes you feel energized and focussed.

That's it!

Fuelling your body can be very simple...if we decide to make it that way. Skip all the marketing and misinformation and start doing what you already know is right!

A SAMPLE WORK FROM HOME DAY

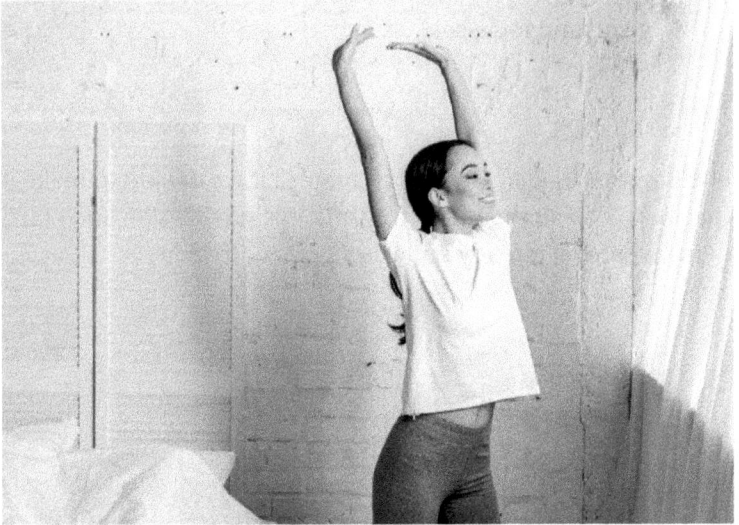

7:00am - Morning routine (Mobility, Breathing, Light Activity, Goals review, Learning, Affirmations, etc.)

7:30am - Shower and change

8:00am - Breakfast

8:15am - Walk around block

8:30am - Working (with Mobility Minute 1-2x per hour)

10:30am - Snack & Mental Health Break (movement/meditation)

10:40am - Working (with Mobility Minute 1-2x per hour)

12:40pm - Lunch & Outdoor Walk

1:30pm - Working (with Mobility Minute 1-2x per hour)

3:30pm - Snack & Mental Health Break (movement/meditation)

3:40pm - Working (with Mobility Minute 1-2x per hour)

5:00pm - Prep for Workout

5:15pm - Workout

6:15pm - Dinner (cook extra for lunch tomorrow and prep tomorrow's snacks)

7:15pm - Relax and chill time with family and friends (video chat or with social distancing protocol)

9:15pm - Start your "Sleep Hygiene Checklist"*

9:45pm - Mobility and breathing

10pm - In bed for sleep

This is merely a sample and your day will look different.

You may choose to do your workout in the morning, at lunch, or modify other aspects of the schedule such as the start, end, and order of activities.

The goal is to show you the key ingredients that should be part of a healthy, active, high performing day, and inspire you to do it.

That's it. The next part is up to you... it is time to put the plan into action!

RELATED RESOURCES

NOTE: *The Sleep Hygiene Checklist and 4 Pillars of Personal Performance (Mindset, Habits, Movement, Fuel) are from the book, "The Fitness Curveball: Hit a Grand Slam in Health and Happiness, No Matter What Life Throws at You".*

Visit www.thefitnesscurveball.com for details, free chapters, or to purchase.

Some important aspects of the sleep hygiene checklist include:
- Turn off all devices and minimize blue light exposure
- Plan tomorrow: "Top 3" and schedule for the day
- Review goals and visualize
- Optimize your room for sleep

NEXT STEPS

You now have the tools to successfully work from home and perhaps even be more productive than you were in the office!

You know what equipment you need, how to set up an effective work environment, what a daily plan should look like, and have the tools to schedule the most important tasks in your day to get more done in less time.

This is just the beginning. The transition to working from home won't be perfect, and may not even be smooth. There will be a lot of mistakes, learning, and some reminders to revisit the foundations of what we've discussed.

The good news is that by implementing these tips, tools, and principles, you will be much more happy and productive than if you didn't!

It's common to have questions, or need help, support, and guidance throughout this challenging time. My team and I are here to help.

We've helped thousands of busy corporate professionals super-charge their health, happiness, productivity, and performance.

When you are ready to start performing at your best, just reach out. Send us an email to info@freshgroup.ca and we will set up a time to chat. No strings attached.

We look forward to connecting with you soon!

Here's to Igniting Your Potential
Tim Borys
CEO
FRESH! Wellness Group

P.S. When you are ready, here are a few ways I can help...

- **PERSONAL: Get FREE Access to my Fitness and Nutrition App**
  This custom designed app provides everything you need for personal health and fitness programming and accountability. Hundreds of free follow-along fitness programs, motivational challenges, community sup-port, fitness and body composition trackers, the ability to ask questions and get answers from my expert coaching team, and other add-on options such as cus-

tomized nutrition, on-demand workouts, live virtual classes, and more! Visit www.freshfitness.ca/app to register for free.

- **PERSONAL: Follow the plan in my book, The Fitness Curvebal**
  This book is your step by step guide to mastering the 4 Pillars of Personal Performance (Mindset, Habits, Movement, Fuel) to look great, feel amazing, reach your goals, and live your best life. *If you are self-motivated, love to read, and ready to change your life, visit www.thefitnesscurveball.com to pick up your copy!*

- **PERSONAL: Join my VIP Coaching Program.**
  This is your chance to work with me one on one, regardless of where you live. Get private coaching in each of the 4 Pillars of performance and leverage my 25+ years of performance coaching experience. Email me *with the word "COACHING" in the subject line and we will set up a quick call to figure out if we are a good fit to work together.*

- **CORPORATE: Workplace Wellness Audit**
  Identify what's working, what's not and receive a valuable report to help you maximize the potential for positive change in your organization. This is a critical first step for any workplace that's serious about improving employee health, happiness, performance, and productivity. Email me *to set up a quick call where we can discuss the details.*

- **CORPORATE: Book Me to Speak to your Company or Corporate Team**
  Choose from many popular topics in the areas of workplace health, performance and engagement, or we will work together to create a custom topic. Email me to set up a quick call where we can discuss the details.

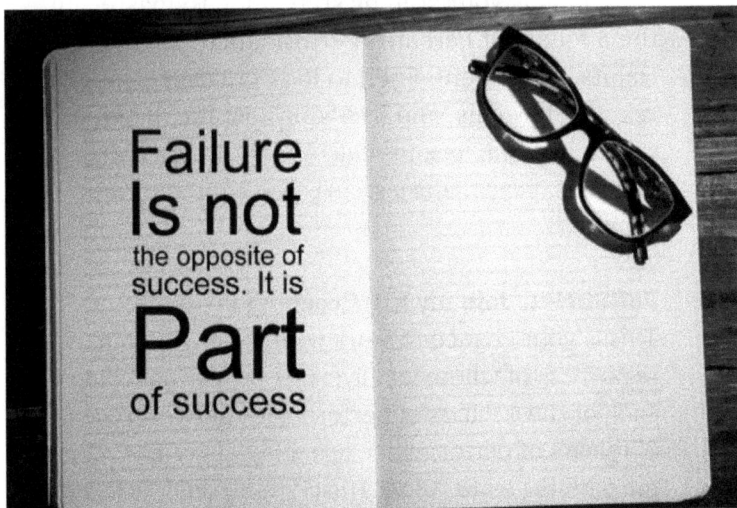

Failure Is not the opposite of success. It is Part of success

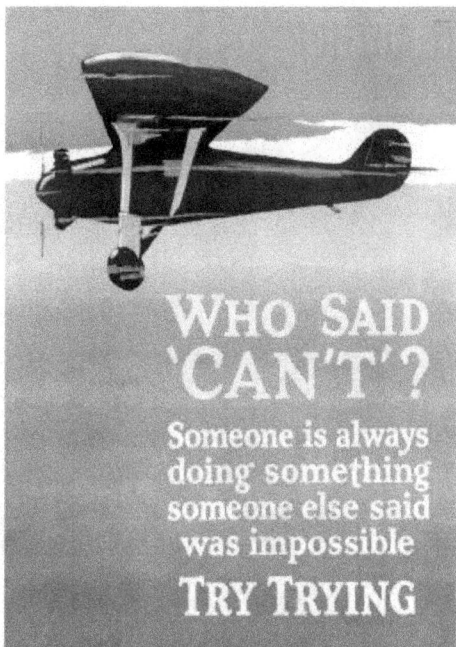

WHO SAID 'CAN'T'?
Someone is always doing something someone else said was impossible
TRY TRYING

ABOUT THE AUTHOR

Tim believes that improved health, happiness and personal performance help us cultivate greatness in our lives and improve the world around us. As a former elite athlete, New York Yankees draft pick, and national level coach, Tim is an expert at eliciting higher performance from individuals and teams. For over 30 years he has helped people and organizations ignite their potential...in work and life. In 2020, he was recognized as one of Canada's Top Trainers.

www.timborys.com
www.thefitnesscurveball.com
www.freshgroup.ca

www.ingramcontent.com/pod-product-compliance
Lightning Source LLC
Chambersburg PA
CBHW060646210326
41520CB00010B/1754